Contents

National Institute of Mental Health

Schizophrenia

What is schizophrenia?

Schizophrenia is a chronic, severe, and disabling brain disorder that has affected people throughout history. About 1 percent of Americans have this illness.[1]

People with the disorder may hear voices other people don't hear. They may believe other people are reading their minds, controlling their thoughts, or plotting to harm them. This can terrify people with the illness and make them withdrawn or extremely agitated.

People with schizophrenia may not make sense when they talk. They may sit for hours without moving or talking. Sometimes people with schizophrenia seem perfectly fine until they talk about what they are really thinking.

Families and society are affected by schizophrenia too. Many people with schizophrenia have difficulty holding a job or caring for themselves, so they rely on others for help.

Treatment helps relieve many symptoms of schizophrenia, but most people who have the disorder cope with symptoms throughout their lives. However, many people with schizophrenia can lead rewarding and meaningful lives in their communities. Researchers are developing more effective medications and using new research tools to understand the causes of schizophrenia. In the years to come, this work may help prevent and better treat the illness.

The symptoms of schizophrenia fall into three broad categories: positive symptoms, negative symptoms, and cognitive symptoms.

Positive symptoms

Positive symptoms are psychotic behaviors not seen in healthy people. People with positive symptoms often "lose touch" with reality. These symptoms can come and go. Sometimes they are severe and at other times hardly noticeable, depending on whether the individual is receiving treatment. They include the following:

Hallucinations are things a person sees, hears, smells, or feels that no one else can see, hear, smell, or feel. "Voices" are the most common type of hallucination in schizophrenia. Many people with the disorder hear voices. The voices may talk to the person about his or her behavior, order the person to do things, or warn the person of danger. Sometimes the voices talk to each other. People with schizophrenia may hear voices for a long time before family and friends notice the problem.

Other types of hallucinations include seeing people or objects that are not there, smelling odors that no one else detects, and feeling things like invisible fingers touching their bodies when no one is near.

Delusions are false beliefs that are not part of the person's culture and do not change. The person believes delusions even after other people prove that the beliefs are not true or logical. People with schizophrenia can have delusions that seem bizarre, such as believing that neighbors can control their behavior with magnetic waves. They may also believe that people on television are directing special messages to them, or that radio stations are broadcasting their thoughts aloud to others. Sometimes they believe they are someone else, such as a famous historical figure. They may have paranoid delusions and believe that others are trying to harm them, such as by cheating, harassing, poisoning, spying on, or plotting against them or the people they care about. These beliefs are called "delusions of persecution."

Thought disorders are unusual or dysfunctional ways of thinking. One form of thought disorder is called "disorganized thinking." This is when a person has trouble organizing his or her thoughts or connecting them logically. They may talk in a garbled way that is hard to understand. Another form is called "thought blocking." This is when a person stops speaking abruptly in the middle of a thought. When asked why he or she stopped talking, the person may say that it felt as if the thought had been taken out of his or her head. Finally, a person with a thought disorder might make up meaningless words, or "neologisms."

Movement disorders may appear as agitated body movements. A person with a movement disorder may repeat certain motions over and over. In the other extreme, a person may become catatonic. Catatonia is a state in which a person does not move and does not respond to others. Catatonia is rare today, but it was more common when treatment for schizophrenia was not available.[2]

Negative symptoms

Negative symptoms are associated with disruptions to normal emotions and behaviors. These symptoms are harder to recognize as part of the disorder and can be mistaken for depression or other conditions. These symptoms include the following:

- "Flat affect" (a person's face does not move or he or she talks in a dull or monotonous voice)

- Lack of pleasure in everyday life

- Lack of ability to begin and sustain planned activities

- Speaking little, even when forced to interact.

People with negative symptoms need help with everyday tasks. They often neglect basic personal hygiene. This may make them seem lazy or unwilling to help themselves, but the problems are symptoms caused by the schizophrenia.

Cognitive symptoms

Cognitive symptoms are subtle. Like negative symptoms, cognitive symptoms may be difficult to recognize as part of the disorder. Often, they are detected only when other tests are performed. Cognitive symptoms include the following:

- Poor "executive functioning" (the ability to understand information and use it to make decisions)

- Trouble focusing or paying attention

- Problems with "working memory" (the ability to use information immediately after learning it).

Cognitive symptoms often make it hard to lead a normal life and earn a living. They can cause great emotional distress.

When does schizophrenia start and who gets it?

Schizophrenia affects men and women equally. It occurs at similar rates in all ethnic groups around the world. Symptoms such as hallucinations and delusions usually start between ages 16 and 30. Men tend to experience symptoms a little earlier than women. Most of the time, people do not get schizophrenia after age 45.[3] Schizophrenia rarely occurs in children, but awareness of childhood-onset schizophrenia is increasing.[4,5]

It can be difficult to diagnose schizophrenia in teens. This is because the first signs can include a change of friends, a drop in grades, sleep problems, and irritability—behaviors that are common among teens. A combination of factors can predict schizophrenia in up to 80 percent of youth who are at high risk of developing the illness. These factors include isolating oneself and withdrawing from others, an increase in unusual thoughts and suspicions, and a family history of psychosis.[6] In young people who develop the disease, this stage of the disorder is called the "prodromal" period.

Are people with schizophrenia violent?

People with schizophrenia are not usually violent. In fact, most violent crimes are not committed by people with schizophrenia.[7] However, some symptoms are associated with violence, such as delusions of persecution. Substance abuse may also increase the chance a person will become violent.[8] If a person with schizophrenia becomes violent, the violence is usually directed at family members and tends to take place at home.

The risk of violence among people with schizophrenia is small. But people with the illness attempt suicide much more often than others. About 10 percent (especially young adult males) die by suicide.[9,10] It is hard to predict which people with schizophrenia are prone to suicide. If you know someone who talks about or attempts suicide, help him or her find professional help right away.

What about substance abuse?

Some people who abuse drugs show symptoms similar to those of schizophrenia. Therefore, people with schizophrenia may be mistaken for people who are affected by drugs. Most researchers do not believe that substance abuse causes schizophrenia. However, people who have schizophrenia are much more likely to have a substance or alcohol abuse problem than the general population.[11]

Substance abuse can make treatment for schizophrenia less effective. Some drugs, like marijuana and stimulants such as amphetamines or cocaine, may make symptoms worse. In fact, research has found increasing evidence of a link between marijuana and schizophrenia symptoms.[12 13] In addition, people who abuse drugs are less likely to follow their treatment plan.

Schizophrenia and smoking

Addiction to nicotine is the most common form of substance abuse in people with schizophrenia. They are addicted to nicotine at three times the rate of the general population (75 to 90 percent vs. 25 to 30 percent).[14]

The relationship between smoking and schizophrenia is complex. People with schizophrenia seem to be driven to smoke, and researchers are exploring whether there is a biological basis for this need. In addition to its known health hazards, several studies have found that smoking may make antipsychotic drugs less effective.

Quitting smoking may be very difficult for people with schizophrenia because nicotine withdrawal may cause their psychotic symptoms to get worse for a while. Quitting strategies that include nicotine replacement methods may be easier for patients to handle. Doctors who treat people with schizophrenia should watch their patients' response to antipsychotic medication carefully if the patient decides to start or stop smoking.

What causes schizophrenia?

Experts think schizophrenia is caused by several factors.

Genes and environment. Scientists have long known that schizophrenia runs in families. The illness occurs in 1 percent of the general population, but it occurs in 10 percent of people who have a first-degree relative with the disorder, such as a parent, brother, or sister. People who have second-degree relatives (aunts, uncles, grandparents, or cousins) with the disease also develop schizophrenia more often than the general population. The risk is highest for an identical twin of a person with schizophrenia. He or she has a 40 to 65 percent chance of developing the disorder.[15]

We inherit our genes from both parents. Scientists believe several genes are associated with an increased risk of schizophrenia, but that no gene causes the disease by itself.[16] In fact, recent research has found that people with schizophrenia tend to have higher rates of rare genetic mutations. These genetic differences involve hundreds of different genes and probably disrupt brain development.[17]

Other recent studies suggest that schizophrenia may result in part when a certain gene that is key to making important brain chemicals malfunctions. This problem may affect the

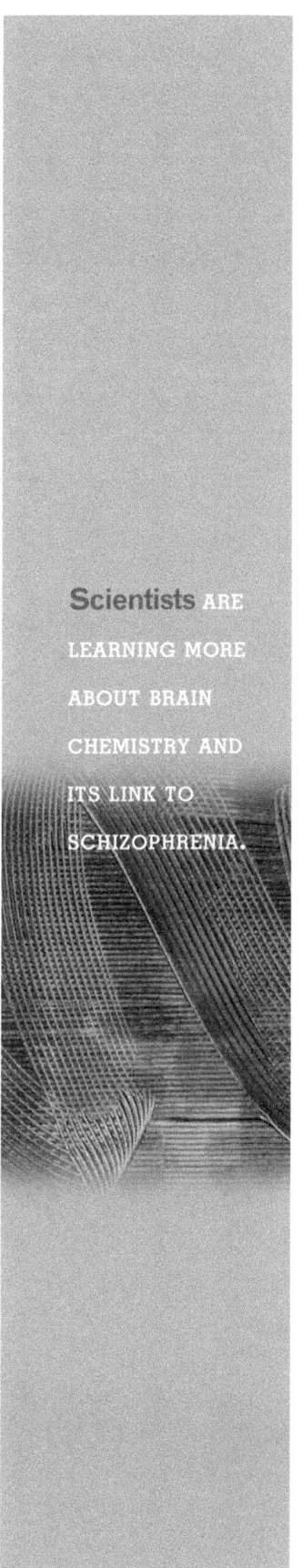

part of the brain involved in developing higher functioning skills.[18] Research into this gene is ongoing, so it is not yet possible to use the genetic information to predict who will develop the disease.

Despite this, tests that scan a person's genes can be bought without a prescription or a health professional's advice. Ads for the tests suggest that with a saliva sample, a company can determine if a client is at risk for developing specific diseases, including schizophrenia. However, scientists don't yet know all of the gene variations that contribute to schizophrenia. Those that are known raise the risk only by very small amounts. Therefore, these "genome scans" are unlikely to provide a complete picture of a person's risk for developing a mental disorder like schizophrenia.

In addition, it probably takes more than genes to cause the disorder. Scientists think interactions between genes and the environment are necessary for schizophrenia to develop. Many environmental factors may be involved, such as exposure to viruses or malnutrition before birth, problems during birth, and other not yet known psychosocial factors.

Different brain chemistry and structure. Scientists think that an imbalance in the complex, interrelated chemical reactions of the brain involving the neurotransmitters dopamine and glutamate, and possibly others, plays a role in schizophrenia. Neurotransmitters are substances that allow brain cells to communicate with each other. Scientists are learning more about brain chemistry and its link to schizophrenia.

Also, in small ways the brains of people with schizophrenia look different than those of healthy people. For example, fluid-filled cavities at the center of the brain, called ventricles, are larger in some people with schizophrenia. The brains of people with the illness also tend to have less gray matter, and some areas of the brain may have less or more activity.

Studies of brain tissue after death also have revealed differences in the brains of people with schizophrenia. Scientists found small changes in the distribution or characteristics of brain cells that likely occurred before birth.[3] Some experts think problems during brain development before birth may lead to faulty connections. The problem may not show up in a person until puberty. The brain undergoes major changes during puberty, and these changes could trigger psychotic symptoms. Scientists have learned a lot about schizophrenia, but more research is needed to help explain how it develops.

How is schizophrenia treated?

Because the causes of schizophrenia are still unknown, treatments focus on eliminating the symptoms of the disease. Treatments include antipsychotic medications and various psychosocial treatments.

Antipsychotic medications

Antipsychotic medications have been available since the mid-1950's. The older types are called conventional or "typical" antipsychotics. Some of the more commonly used typical medications include:

- Chlorpromazine (Thorazine)

- Haloperidol (Haldol)

- Perphenazine (Etrafon, Trilafon)

- Fluphenazine (Prolixin).

In the 1990's, new antipsychotic medications were developed. These new medications are called second generation, or "atypical" antipsychotics.

One of these medications, clozapine (Clozaril) is an effective medication that treats psychotic symptoms, hallucinations, and breaks with reality. But clozapine can sometimes cause a serious problem called agranulocytosis, which is a loss of the white blood cells that help a person fight infection. People who take clozapine must get their white blood cell counts checked every week or two. This problem and the cost of

blood tests make treatment with clozapine difficult for many people. But clozapine is potentially helpful for people who do not respond to other antipsychotic medications.[19]

Other atypical antipsychotics were also developed. None cause agranulocytosis. Examples include:

- Risperidone (Risperdal)

- Olanzapine (Zyprexa)

- Quetiapine (Seroquel)

- Ziprasidone (Geodon)

- Aripiprazole (Abilify)

- Paliperidone (Invega).

What are the side effects?
Some people have side effects when they start taking these medications. Most side effects go away after a few days and often can be managed successfully. People who are taking antipsychotics should not drive until they adjust to their new medication. Side effects of many antipsychotics include:

- Drowsiness

- Dizziness when changing positions

- Blurred vision

- Rapid heartbeat

- Sensitivity to the sun

- Skin rashes

- Menstrual problems for women.

Atypical antipsychotic medications can cause major weight gain and changes in a person's metabolism. This may increase a person's risk of getting diabetes and high cholesterol.[20] A person's weight, glucose levels, and lipid levels should be monitored regularly by a doctor while taking an atypical antipsychotic medication.

Scientists HAVE LEARNED A LOT ABOUT SCHIZOPHRENIA, BUT MORE RESEARCH IS NEEDED TO HELP EXPLAIN HOW IT DEVELOPS.

Typical antipsychotic medications can cause side effects related to physical movement, such as:

- Rigidity

- Persistent muscle spasms

- Tremors

- Restlessness.

Long-term use of typical antipsychotic medications may lead to a condition called tardive dyskinesia (TD). TD causes muscle movements a person can't control. The movements commonly happen around the mouth. TD can range from mild to severe, and in some people the problem cannot be cured. Sometimes people with TD recover partially or fully after they stop taking the medication.

TD happens to fewer people who take the atypical antipsychotics, but some people may still get TD. People who think that they might have TD should check with their doctor before stopping their medication.

How are antipsychotics taken and how do people respond to them?

Antipsychotics are usually in pill or liquid form. Some anti-psychotics are shots that are given once or twice a month.

Symptoms of schizophrenia, such as feeling agitated and having hallucinations, usually go away within days. Symptoms like delusions usually go away within a few weeks. After about six weeks, many people will see a lot of improvement.

However, people respond in different ways to antipsychotic medications, and no one can tell beforehand how a person will respond. Sometimes a person needs to try several medications before finding the right one. Doctors and patients can work together to find the best medication or medication combination, as well as the right dose.

Some people may have a relapse—their symptoms come back or get worse. Usually, relapses happen when people stop taking their medication, or when they only take it sometimes.

Some people stop taking the medication because they feel better or they may feel they don't need it anymore. But no one should stop taking an antipsychotic medication without talking to his or her doctor. When a doctor says it is okay to stop taking a medication, it should be gradually tapered off, never stopped suddenly.

How do antipsychotics interact with other medications?

Antipsychotics can produce unpleasant or dangerous side effects when taken with certain medications. For this reason, all doctors treating a patient need to be aware of all the medications that person is taking. Doctors need to know about prescription and over-the-counter medicine, vitamins, minerals, and herbal supplements. People also need to discuss any alcohol or other drug use with their doctor.

To find out more about how antipsychotics work, the National Institute of Mental Health (NIMH) funded a study called CATIE (Clinical Antipsychotic Trials of Intervention Effectiveness). This study compared the effectiveness and side effects of five antipsychotics used to treat people with schizophrenia. In general, the study found that the older typical antipsychotic perphenazine (Trilafon) worked as well as the newer, atypical medications. But because people respond differently to different medications, it is important that treatments be designed carefully for each person. More information about CATIE is on the NIMH Web site at http://www.nimh.nih.gov/health/trials/practical/catie/index.shtml.

Psychosocial treatments

Psychosocial treatments can help people with schizophrenia who are already stabilized on antipsychotic medication. Psychosocial treatments help these patients deal with the everyday challenges of the illness, such as difficulty with communication, self-care, work, and forming and keeping relationships. Learning and using coping mechanisms to address these problems allow people with schizophrenia to socialize and attend school and work.

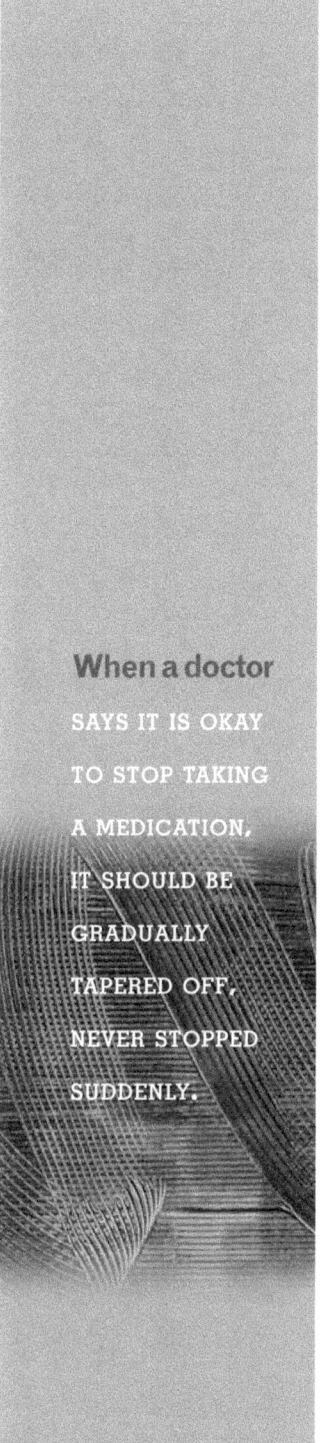

When a doctor SAYS IT IS OKAY TO STOP TAKING A MEDICATION, IT SHOULD BE GRADUALLY TAPERED OFF, NEVER STOPPED SUDDENLY.

Patients who receive regular psychosocial treatment also are more likely to keep taking their medication, and they are less likely to have relapses or be hospitalized. A therapist can help patients better understand and adjust to living with schizophrenia. The therapist can provide education about the disorder, common symptoms or problems patients may experience, and the importance of staying on medications. For more information on psychosocial treatments, see the psychotherapies section on the NIMH Web site at http://www.nimh.nih.gov/health/topics/psychotherapies/index.shtml.

Illness management skills. People with schizophrenia can take an active role in managing their own illness. Once patients learn basic facts about schizophrenia and its treatment, they can make informed decisions about their care. If they know how to watch for the early warning signs of relapse and make a plan to respond, patients can learn to prevent relapses. Patients can also use coping skills to deal with persistent symptoms.

Integrated treatment for co-occurring substance abuse. Substance abuse is the most common co-occurring disorder in people with schizophrenia. But ordinary substance abuse treatment programs usually do not address this population's special needs. When schizophrenia treatment programs and drug treatment programs are used together, patients get better results.

Rehabilitation. Rehabilitation emphasizes social and vocational training to help people with schizophrenia function better in their communities. Because schizophrenia usually develops in people during the critical career-forming years of life (ages 18 to 35), and because the disease makes normal thinking and functioning difficult, most patients do not receive training in the skills needed for a job.

Rehabilitation programs can include job counseling and training, money management counseling, help in learning to use public transportation, and opportunities to practice communication skills. Rehabilitation programs work well when

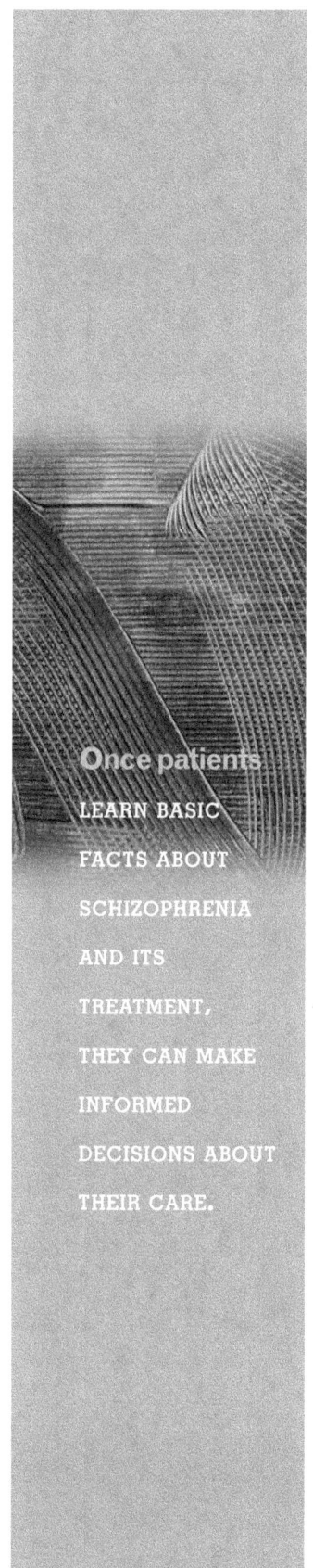

they include both job training and specific therapy designed to improve cognitive or thinking skills. Programs like this help patients hold jobs, remember important details, and improve their functioning.[21,22,23]

Family education. People with schizophrenia are often discharged from the hospital into the care of their families. So it is important that family members know as much as possible about the disease. With the help of a therapist, family members can learn coping strategies and problem-solving skills. In this way the family can help make sure their loved one sticks with treatment and stays on his or her medication. Families should learn where to find outpatient and family services.

Cognitive behavioral therapy. Cognitive behavioral therapy (CBT) is a type of psychotherapy that focuses on thinking and behavior. CBT helps patients with symptoms that do not go away even when they take medication. The therapist teaches people with schizophrenia how to test the reality of their thoughts and perceptions, how to "not listen" to their voices, and how to manage their symptoms overall. CBT can help reduce the severity of symptoms and reduce the risk of relapse.

Self-help groups. Self-help groups for people with schizophrenia and their families are becoming more common. Professional therapists usually are not involved, but group members support and comfort each other. People in self-help groups know that others are facing the same problems, which can help everyone feel less isolated. The networking that takes place in self-help groups can also prompt families to work together to advocate for research and more hospital and community treatment programs. Also, groups may be able to draw public attention to the discrimination many people with mental illnesses face.

How can you help a person with schizophrenia?

People with schizophrenia can get help from professional case managers and caregivers at residential or day programs. However, family members usually are a patient's primary caregivers.

People with schizophrenia often resist treatment. They may not think they need help because they believe their delusions or hallucinations are real. In these cases, family and friends may need to take action to keep their loved one safe. Laws vary from state to state, and it can be difficult to force a person with a mental disorder into treatment or hospitalization. But when a person becomes dangerous to himself or herself, or to others, family members or friends may have to call the police to take their loved one to the hospital.

Treatment at the hospital. In the emergency room, a mental health professional will assess the patient and determine whether a voluntary or involuntary admission is needed. For a person to be admitted involuntarily, the law states that the professional must witness psychotic behavior and hear the person voice delusional thoughts. Family and friends can provide needed information to help a mental health professional make a decision.

After a loved one leaves the hospital. Family and friends can help their loved ones get treatment and take their medication once they go home. If patients stop taking their medication or stop going to follow-up appointments, their symptoms likely will return. Sometimes symptoms become severe for people who stop their medication and treatment. This is dangerous, since they may become unable to care for themselves. Some people end up on the street or in jail, where they rarely receive the kind of help they need.

People with SCHIZOPHRENIA CAN GET HELP FROM PROFESSIONAL CASE MANAGERS AND CAREGIVERS AT RESIDENTIAL OR DAY PROGRAMS.

Family and friends can also help patients set realistic goals and learn to function in the world. Each step toward these goals should be small and taken one at a time. The patient will need support during this time. When people with a mental illness are pressured and criticized, they usually do not get well. Often, their symptoms may get worse. Telling them when they are doing something right is the best way to help them move forward.

It can be difficult to know how to respond to someone with schizophrenia who makes strange or clearly false statements. Remember that these beliefs or hallucinations seem very real to the person. It is not helpful to say they are wrong or imaginary. But going along with the delusions is not helpful, either. Instead, calmly say that you see things differently. Tell them that you acknowledge that everyone has the right to see things his or her own way. In addition, it is important to understand that schizophrenia is a biological illness. Being respectful, supportive, and kind without tolerating dangerous or inappropriate behavior is the best way to approach people with this disorder.

What is the outlook for the future?

The outlook for people with schizophrenia continues to improve. Although there is no cure, treatments that work well are available. Many people with schizophrenia improve enough to lead independent, satisfying lives.

Continued research and understanding in genetics, neuroscience, and behavioral science will help scientists and health professionals understand the causes of the disorder and how it may be predicted and prevented. This work will help experts develop better treatments to help people with schizophrenia achieve their full potential. Families and individuals who are living with schizophrenia are encouraged to participate in clinical research. For up-to-date information about the latest NIMH-funded research in schizophrenia, see the NIMH Web site at http://www.nimh.nih.gov.

Citations

1. Regier DA, Narrow WE, Rae DS, Manderscheid RW, Locke BZ, Goodwin FK. The de facto US mental and addictive disorders service system. Epidemiologic catchment area prospective 1-year prevalence rates of disorders and services. *Archives of General Psychiatry*. 1993 Feb;50(2):85-94.

2. World Health Organization (WHO). Catatonic Schizophrenia. The ICD-10 Classification of Mental and Behavioural Disorders: Clinical descriptions and diagnostic guidelines.1992.Geneva, Switzerland: World Health Organization.

3. Mueser KT and McGurk SR. Schizophrenia. *Lancet*. 2004 Jun 19;363(9426):2063-2072.

4. Nicolson R, Lenane M, Hamburger SD, Fernandez T, Bedwell J, Rapoport JL. Lessons from childhood-onset schizophrenia. *Brain Research Review*. 2000;31(2-3):147-156.

5. Masi G, Mucci M, Pari C. Children with schizophrenia: clinical picture and pharmacological treatment. *CNS Drugs*. 2006;20(10):841-866.

6. Cannon TD, Cadenhead K, Cornblatt B, Woods SW, Addington J, Walker E, Seidman LJ, Perkins D, Tsuang M, McGlashan T, Heinssen R. Prediction of psychosis in high-risk youth: A Multi-site longitudinal study in North America. *Archives of General Psychiatry*. 2008 Jan;65(1):28-37.

7. Walsh E, Buchanan A, Fahy T. Violence and schizophrenia: examining the evidence. *British Journal of Psychiatry*. 2002 Jun;180:490-495.

8. Swanson JW, Swartz MS, Van Dorn RA, Elbogen E, Wager HR, Rosenheck RA, Stroup S, McEvoy JP, Lieberman JA. A national study of violent behavior in persons with schizophrenia. *Archives of General Psychiatry*. 2006 May;63(5):490-499.

9. Meltzer HY, Alphs L, Green AI, Altamura AC, Anand R, Bertoldi A, Bourgeois M, Chouinard G, Islam MZ, Kane J, Krishnan R, Lindenmayer JP, Potkin S, International Suicide Prevention Trial Study Group. Clozapine treatment for suicidality in schizophrenia: International Suicide Prevention Trial (InterSePT). *Archives of General Psychiatry*. 2003 Jan;60(1):82-91.

10. Meltzer HY and Baldessarini RJ. Reducing the risk for suicide in schizophrenia and affective disorders. *Journal of Clinical Psychiatry*. 2003 Sep;64(9):1122-1129.

11. Blanchard JJ, Brown SA, Horan WP, Sherwood AR. Substance use disorders in schizophrenia: Reviews, integration and a proposed model. *Clinical Psychological Review*. 2000;20:207-234.

12. Zullino DF, Waber L, Khazaal Y. Cannabis and the course of schizophrenia. *American Journal of Psychiatry*. 2008;165(10):1357-1358.

13. Muller-Vahl KR and Emrich HM. Cannabis and schizophrenia: towards a cannabinoid hypothesis of schizophrenia. *Expert Review of Neurotherapeutics*. 2008;8(7):1037-1048.

14. Jones RT and Benowitz NL. Therapeutics for Nicotine Addiction. In Davis KL, Charney D, Coyle JT & Nemeroff C (Eds.), Neuropsychopharmacology: The Fifth Generation of Progress (pp1533-1544). 2002. Nashville, TN:American College of Neuropsychopharmacology.

15. Cardno AG and Gottesman II. Twin studies of schizophrenia: from bow-and-arrow concordances to star wars Mx and functional genomics. *American Journal of Medical Genetics*. 2000 Spring;97(1):12-17.

16. Harrison PJ and Weinberger DR. Schizophrenia genes, gene expression, and neuropathology: on the matter of their convergence. *Molecular Psychiatry.* 2005;10(1):40-68.

17. Walsh T, McClellan JM, McCarthy SE, Addington AM, Pierce SB, Cooper GM, Nord AS, Kusenda M, Malhotra D, Bhandari A, Stray SM, Rippey CF, Roccanova P, Makarov V, Lakshmi B, Findling RL, Sikich L, Stromberg T, Merriman B, Gogtay N, Butler P, Eckstrand K, Noory L, Gochman P, Long R, Chen Z, Davis S, Baker C, Eichler EE, Meltzer PS, Nelson SF, Singleton AB, Lee MK, Rapoport JL, King MC, Sebat J. Rare structural variants disrupt multiple genes in neurodevelopmental pathways in schizophrenia. *Science.* 2008 Apr 25;320(5875):539-543.

18. Huang HS, Matevossian A, Whittle C, Kim SY, Schumacher A, Baker SP, Akbarian S. Prefrontal dysfunction in schizophrenia involves missed-lineage leukemia 1-regulated histone methylation at GABAergic gene promoters. *Journal of Neuroscience.* 2007 Oct 17;27(42):11254-11262.

19. Gogtay N and Rapoport J. Clozapine use in children and adolescents. *Expert Opinion on Pharmacotherapy.* 2008;9(3):459-465.

20. Lieberman JA, Stroup TS, McEvoy JP, Swartz MS, Rosenheck RA, Perkins DO, Keefe RS, Davis SM, Davis CE, Lebowitz BD, Severe J, Hsiao JK, Clinical Antipsychotic Trials of Intervention Effectiveness (CATIE). Effectiveness of antipsychotic drugs in patients with chronic schizophrenia. *New England Journal of Medicine.* 2005 Sep 22;353(12):1209-1223.

21. Greig TC, Zito W, Wexler BE, Fiszdon J, Bell MD. Improved cognitive function in schizophrenia after one year of cognitive training and vocational services. *Schizophrenia Research.* 2007 Nov;96(1-3):156-161.

22. Bell M, Fiszon J, Greig T, Wexler B, Bryson G. Neurocognitive enhancement therapy with work therapy in schizophrenia: 6-month follow-up of neuropsychological performance. *Journal of Rehabilitation Research and Development.* 2007;44(5):761-770.

23. Hogarty GE, Flesher S, Ulrich R, Carter M, Greenwald D, Poque-Geile M, Kechavan M, Cooley S, DiBarry AL, Garrett A, Parepally H, Zoretich R. Cognitive enhancement therapy for schizophrenia: effects of a 2-year randomized trial on cognition and behavior. *Archives of General Psychiatry.* 2004 Sep;61(9):866-876.

For more information on schizophrenia

Visit the National Library of Medicine's MedlinePlus
   http://medlineplus.gov
   En Español, **http://medlineplus.gov/spanish**

For information on clinical trials for schizophrenia
   http://www.nimh.nih.gov/health/trials/index.shtml

National Library of Medicine Clinical Trials Database
   http://www.clinicaltrials.gov

Clinical trials at NIMH in Bethesda, MD
   http://patientinfo.nimh.nih.gov or call 1-888-674-6464

Information from NIMH is available in multiple formats. You can browse online, download documents in PDF, and order paper brochures through the mail. If you would like to have NIMH publications, you can order them online at **http://www.nimh.nih.gov**. If you do not have Internet access and wish to have information that supplements this publication, please contact the NIMH Information Resource Center at the numbers listed below.

National Institute of Mental Health
Science Writing, Press & Dissemination Branch
6001 Executive Boulevard
Room 8184, MSC 9663
Bethesda, MD 20892-9663
Phone: 301-443-4513 or
1-866-615-NIMH (6464) toll-free
TTY: 301-443-8431 or
1-866-415-8051 toll-free
FAX: 301-443-4279
E-mail: nimhinfo@nih.gov
Web site: **http://www.nimh.nih.gov**

Reprints

NIMH publications are in the public domain and may be reproduced or copied without permission from the National Institute of Mental Health. NIMH encourages you to reproduce them and use them in your efforts to improve public health. Citation of the National Institute of Mental Health as a source is appreciated. However, using government materials inappropriately can raise legal or ethical concerns, so we ask you to use these guidelines:

- NIMH does not endorse or recommend any commercial products, processes, or services, and publications may not be used for advertising or endorsement purposes.

- NIMH does not provide specific medical advice or treatment recommendations or referrals; these materials may not be used in a manner that has the appearance of such information.

- NIMH requests that non-Federal organizations not alter publications in a way that will jeopardize the integrity and "brand" when using publications.

- Addition of non-Federal Government logos and Web site links may not have the appearance of NIMH endorsement of any specific commercial products or services or medical treatments or services.

If you have questions regarding these guidelines and use of NIMH publications, please contact the NIMH Information Resource Center at 1-866-615-6464 or e-mail at nimhinfo@nih.gov.